D1588376

THE
COLLECTED
POEMS OF
GEORGE
BRUCE

1939 – 70

THE
COLLECTED
POEMS OF
GEORGE
BRUCE

at the
University Press

EDINBURGH

Printed in Great Britain
by W & J Mackay & Co Ltd, Chatham

Contents

🌿 Sea Talk

Contents

Contents

Contents

FOR
ELIZABETH
MY WIFE

A skull shoots sea-green grass from its sockets.
I saw it as the wave lengthened and flattened.
Moon whitened the cranium, plied its beams upon
The shooting sea green hair.

> You tell me not to stare
> So in upon myself
> Nor throw the arc-light
> Of the mind.

> But here my songs begin
> Here their first thin irregular,
> (Like the waver of the wind)
> Yet sometimes taut, music.

The oar rots on the beach.
The skua breeds on the cliff.

> A song for Scotland this,
> For the people
> Of the clearances,
> For the dead tenements,
> For the dead herring
> On the living water.
> A song for Scotland this.

This which I write now
Was written years ago
Before my birth
In the features of my father.

It was stamped
In the rock formations
West of my hometown.
Not I write,

But, perhaps William Bruce,
Cooper.
Perhaps here his hand
Well articled in his trade.

Then though my words
Hit out
An ebullition from
City or flower,

There not my faith,
These the paint
Smeared upon
The inarticulate,

The salt crusted sea-boot,
The red-eyed mackerel,
The plate shining with herring,
And many men,

Seamen and craftsmen and curers,
And behind them
The protest of hundreds of years,
The sea obstinate against the land.

My House

My house
Is granite
It fronts
North,

Where the Firth flows,
East the sea.
My room
holds the first

Blow from the North,
The first from East,
Salt upon
The pane.

In the dark
I, a child,
Did not know
The consuming night

And heard
The wind,
Unworried and
Warm—secure.

Half way up the stairs
Is the tall curtain.
We noticed it there
After the unfinished tale.

My father came home,
His clothes sea-wet,
His breath cold.
He said a boat had gone.

He held a lantern.
The mist moved in,
Rested on the stone step
And hung above the floor.

I remembered
The blue glint
Of the herring scales
Fixed in the mat,

And also a foolish crab
That held his own pincers fast.
We called him
Old Iron-clad.

I smelt again
The kippers cooked in oak ash.
That helped me to forget
The tall curtain.

In summer the sky
Was lit late.
Nearby the beach
Were stalls, swing boats,

Steam driven round-abouts
Gold horses of wood
Or bright red chair-o-planes
And mechanical music.

On the links stood
A boxing booth.
'Boys half price for the boxing.'
The fishermen spent money here.

Here Rob Burke was at work
Taking all comers
Till dark.
He put the finger of his glove

To his flat nose, snorted,
And then spat.
Short work was made of
Our Tom Scott.

We saw even the dust rise.
Outside the land was black.
'That's queer' I said,
'Sea's lit—like a lamp.'

Boys on knees, or prostrate, and scrambling
About rocks, by rock pools and inlets,
Noting with accurate eye the wash of water.
They hunt (O primitives!) for small fish,
Inches long only, and quicksilver,
But pink beneath the dorsal fin
Moving with superb locomotion.
Bodies bent, eyes all upon the prey—
Boys in shallow water with sun-warmed feet.

The Startled Hare

Hare leaps with eye of fear.
Sparse grass, sanded and salt, prompts.
And air—what daylight here!—
Through limb and limb cavorts.

Dust puffs at feet: he lollops free,
Where tern astride, or winging on, a minor breeze
Stares to the wind abundant sea.
This winter too before gorse breaks and beams.

Space!—here runs astringent air
Across the loch fixed
In three miles of flat,
The habitat of thistle and hare.

Outpaced gull and tern
Swing in a catspaw's fuff.
By the shocked occasional tree
Wind twists to the fern.

Cower weasel in the wall,
Look upon our scenery.
The loch fixed
Tree torn from soil.

The Town

Between the flat land of the plain
And the brief rock—the town.
This morning the eye receives
(As if the space had not intervened,
As if white light of extraordinary transparency
Had conveyed it silent and with smooth vigour)
The granite edge, edifice of stone—
The new tenement takes the sun.
The shop fronts stare,
The church spire signals heaven,
The blue-tarred streets divide and open sea-ward,
The air leaps like an animal.

Did once the sea engulf all here and then
At second thought withdraw to leave
A sea-washed town?

I go North to cold, to home, to Kinnaird,
Fit monument for our time.

This is the outermost edge of Buchan.
Inland the sea birds range,
The tree's leaf has salt upon it,
The tree turns to the low stone wall.
And here a promontory rises towards Norway.
Irregular to the top of thin grey grass
Where the spindrift in storm lays it beads.
The water plugs in the cliff sides,
The gull cries from the clouds
This is the consummation of the plain.

O impregnable and very ancient rock,
Rejecting the violence of water,
Ignoring its accumulations and strategy,
You yield to history nothing.

1 THE WINE TOWER

Now our poverty when most we need the Canon of a Giant Art,
That will contain disruption. What shape of life
Dare we to propagate in History?—An image
Holds the mind. A blind tower upon a basalt floor
Lips cliff, both subject to the force of air and sea.
This cube was the repository of wine for Frazer of Saltoun.
Fine wine. One took it upon the tips of alert senses,
Savoured it on palate and by intellect. So *we* present at once
To the unbound future, the supple muscle and the exquisitely
                                          receptive nerve.

2 TOWER AND CASTLE

Violence without, within legend. Years ago the empty barrels
Roistered doon the braes. The castle wis lit,
An' extra men were put to roll more wine from tower
To hoose that stood well back ahint the cliff.
They say that more matured than wine therein. The dark
Once prisoned the old man's daughter wha' wantit
The wrang man: an' ballad like, the pointed rock aneath.
Had her. Her songsters were the gulls.

3 THE CASTLE TURNED LIGHTHOUSE

The present occupant of the house attends a new plant,
Powerful machinery operating to project a beam of light
For ten miles. Ball bearing, frictionless lamp—
What immeasurable skill upon a thing!
As if the subtleties of the brain were taken out
And we left only to be minders of the machine,
Admirers of our suicide.

This is the land without myth—
From the crown of this low hill
To the useful country receding East
To the rectangular towns we have built;
Coast towns, granite pavemented, with drinking troughs
For the animals, electric standards, kiosks,
Large gasometers and excellent sanitation.
Parks and tennis courts are at the disposal
Of the young, and at the sea, gaiety,
Almost a semi-circle of amusement
Extending invitations to all couples,
At least in summer—but not (as you know)
This year though the sunlight remains
Astride the promenade and pier.
This is the land without myth.

Then all was idleness, and wealth
Like sand, or so it seemed,
Spread in the uncles' cars upon the beach.
Have the bazaars closed down,
And for us between the sea and the land
No prizes? Waste.
This is the land without myth.

The crab scuttles on the sea floor,
Hook dangles, net opens to the tide,
The boat's keel is still or moves
With the greater water movement.
Between the thumb and the first finger
The weighted line.

Look inland beyond the roof tops, behind
The allotments and the tin sheds.
(This is the land without myth.)
The coulter is in the soil,
The thin crop is on the iron rock
The field glitters like a new coin.

Here are neither mountains nor dark valleys
Here the shadow's length is man, or the tree
That is his, or the house he has built.
Years back the stones were lifted from the fields,
The animals driven to their holes, the land drained,
Dug, planted, the ground pieced out.
The heather was beat. The crop grew
On the hill. The paths were trod.
The land was peopled and tilled.
This is the land without myth.

By the burn the children collect
Small blue butterflies. The poppies are theirs.
For them the sun stands at attention,
The road stretches out in its blueness,
Their feet clatter upon it.
This is a known land,
A land without myth.

to a Buchan Fisherman

1   Night holds the past, the present is manifest in day,
In day activity, but night shuts the door—
And within the mind hints of your old powers,
Recollections of your associate, the sea.

Now this night in tribute I write you
And have you, your boys, your wife in mind
The better for not being there where you are.
Too much business there with winch running,
Pulleys slipping, hawsers, horses, men, lorries, herring;
Besides, being a cranner I must note the fish
And see to the salt. But here
I remember again your boys on the beach at sun-down,
Their graips at sods of sand,
Their hands' flash for bait,
Behind—sandhills with grass,
In front the sea, that sea that binds to it
The cottage on the cliff top or on the shore,
Invades the ears of the boy, enters his eyes, binds him
And the crustacea—monsters of the sea pools.

Consider the spider crab.
From the rock, half rock itself, pinhead eyes project,
The mechanism of movement awkward, legs propelled
A settlement for parasite, for limpet;
Passionless stone in the world of motion.
The pounded shells, a broken razor,
Mussel, fan, speak as much life.
O dark haired fisherman who know the tides
And proper prices for the catch,
Here is the image of your skull.
Who will tell upon the shingle beach
Which the shell splinter, which the particle of the skull
Long bleached by the flow and ebb?

The sea binds the village,
Its salt constricts the pasture behind,

Its gale fastens the bent grass before,
Its fog is in the nostrils of the boy.
Your iron ship, a novelty to sea's age,
Puts out. Sea gives tongue to greater
Fears, deeds, terrors, than you can tell.
It's articulate in the crab, the hermit, spider, partan.
These tell the knowledge in your bone,
Over these your boat slips
And down to these grope line and nets.
Here breed the initiates of life
In rock chambers and on the floor beneath tide,
Beneath sway and trouble, undisturbed.

2   Of Balbec and Finistère Proust wrote—
The oldest bone in the earth's skeleton,
The land's end of France, Europe, of the Old World,
The ultimate encampment of fishermen
Who since the beginning faced
The everlasting kingdom of fog,
Of shadows of the night. Coast
Contemporaneous with the great geological phenomena,
Remote from human history as the constellations.
And here upon a promontory
At the foot of the cliffs of Death,
Not, as might have been expected,
The timid essay towards life,
Nor yet a bastion threatening the sea's force,
But, peculiar growth on these rocks,
The tender Gothic with a spire flowering;
Below it the blunt stone faced apostles,
And at the porch the Virgin:
Enveloping all—salt fog.

To defend life thus and so to grace it
What art! but you, my friend, know nothing of this,
Merely the fog, more often the east wind
That scours the sand from the shore,

Bequeathing it to the sheep pasture,
Whipping the dust from fields,
Disclosing the stone ribs of earth—
The frame that for ever presses back the roots of corn
In the shallow soil. This wind,
Driving over your roof,
Twists the sycamore's branches,
Till its dwarf fingers shoot west,
Outspread on bare country, lying wide.
Erect against the element
House and kirk and your flint face.

The kirk looks graceless, a block house
To defy the last snort of winter,
The house shouldering the sea,
Dark as your ship inside, the windows locked,
The curtains heavy as if suspecting light.
Both bar the element, shut, as your face is shut,
To the subtle invaders, to fortune the anarchist
To the spies of Spring, to the lecher in the blood.

3   Your face burgeons before me out of night,
Blue jowled, nose aquiline, big mouth,
Fisher grey eyes with resolute and phlegmatic look.
Nor do these features tell all the sea story
And in imagination blossoms that angular, garrulous man
Who skippered the Gem, matching your ease
With his reckless tongue. His name was Gatt:
Lithe, restless, drunken, bigoted, but like you too
Accepting the thump and peril of water.
Both hammered between these—poles apart—
Water and the Word—both gifts of God.

Between these your feet are shaped, your hands helped
By water, pebble, cliff and sky.
Blue rocks nose above the sand about your feet,
Feet expert and attentive to the ship's swing.
Your hands like women's in their dexterity,

Never fumble needle or net, rope or wheel.
Their clutch is taught by the sea's clutch,
The small words of sea talk, the mumbling
And knocking at the little boat's side,
These pleasantries teach and the rest,
The unforgettable clap making even you merely awkward,
A doll only in a doll's house put together.

This is the gift of God.
Accept the road your feet have taken
Over the pebbles to the pier, from pier to deck boards.
You have seven paces on board, seven on return, no more,
Turning inward lest the sea have you.
Accept the sublit seas beneath—the squid,
The pink and purple prostrates, valvular jellies,
Fungoid jungle. Here globe, tube, cone, the final shapes
Have life, have mouths, erupt, move in currents
Without air and are still—lives crepuscular.
With these lands I have no acquaintance.
Accept them as you accept
The little fish leaping in the morning
From the net streaming into the scuppers.

Your life is strife,
Your nose has long snuffed wind harsh with salt,
You have seen plenty sour mornings,
But the day you took that shot to port—herring deck high—
Was fine, blowy and with sun. Cloud from the North
Piled up by the foremast and beat off fast South.
The gulls knew you were heavy loaded,
Met and escorted you,
Swinging just over you in the trough,
Just over you on the swell.
The boat's bow pressed on the water,
Under the stern the sea blackened,
The wave flattened out, but, resilient and very powerful,
Pushed at the strakes and hull.
The propeller forced water into spirals widening at the top,

Their track broadened behind,
Fell away, and mixed with expanse.
Did luck or judgment make that catch?
'Fifty mile oot aff Sumburgh Head'—the night airy
The moon behind fine cloud, some motion.

Certainty of hand despite the numbing night,
Sureness of feet despite the deck at odds with them,
Knowledge of course from compass and stars;
What conjunction brought success?
You know how sweet
To attribute success to the skill of eye and hands and feet,
How difficult
To walk with circumspection between pride and despair.

Do you not despair of the unspeculating eyes of fish,
Of the ignorance of oceans,
Of the infinite varieties of species
Articulating in their variety, indifference,
Creating to perish, perishing to create
The continuing indifferent sea face?

'Who hath measured the waters in the hollow of his hand
And meted out heaven with the span
And comprehended the dust of the earth in a measure
And weighed the mountain in the scales
And the hill in a balance?

Have ye not known? Have ye not heard?
Hath it not been told you from the beginning?
Have ye not understood from the foundations of the earth?'

My dead father speaks to me
In a look he wore when dying.
The emaciated hands and limbs
Pass from the memory,
But that mask appropriate to that moment
When he balanced between two worlds
Remains to rise again and again
Like an unanswered question.

He was going very fast then
To be distributed amongst the things
And creatures of the ground and sea.
He was ready for the shells and worms,
(Outside the rain stormed
And the small boats at the pier jolted)
His eyes had passed to the other side
Of terror and pain.

Night had settled in each.
The dissipation of feature,
The manifestation of skull,
The lengthening of cheek,
The dark filtering into the hollows,
Told *one* thing:
What speed towards our mother!

But another image here too,
Something I had seen before
Caverned in the El Greco face,
Something presented to us
From the other side of dream;
Translatable only in hints from the breathless world.

There is no home for the hero.
Even when a boy he left his passions
At the pier. His eyes did not note them,
Nor the white handkerchiefs, but turned,
As the North controlled needle turns,
To the gulls who offered no memento.

Yet with the rest he had his curios,
The master key that opened all,
The starfish sporting one more limb,
The match-box with the double back,
Shells highly convoluted like a screw,
But these made exits from his heart.

And school was taken in his stride,
His gaze averted from it all,
Though capes and bays and distances
Were glanced at, recognised
As matters of potential interest.
Astronomy he was not taught.

Darkness ingathers the ship. The foam
Of many seas arches upon her bows.
The cargoes, corn for metal,
Make their change. And he takes stock,
Sees to delivery, hears the engine run,
And stands observant at the winch.

There is no home for the hero.
His head—like a head in profile,
The minted head on a coin—
Occupies the windy spaces
And holds predestined courses.

As he comes from one of those small houses
Set within the curve of the low cliff
For a moment he pauses
Foot on step at the low lintel
Before fronting wind and sun.
He carries out from within something of the dark
Concealed by heavy curtain,
Or held within the ship under hatches.

Yet with what assurance
The compact body moves,
Head pressed to wind,
His being at an angle
As to anticipate the lurch of earth.

Who is he to contain night
And still walk stubborn
Holding the ground with light feet
And with a careless gait?
Perhaps a cataract of light floods,
Perhaps the apostolic flame.
Whatever it may be
The road takes him from us.
Now the pier is his, now the tide.

The needle starts North.
There the still simplicity in the single gull
That hangs above the rock,
Or in the stone of the low wall, a shelter
For the wiry animals, or in stone
Of granite quarried in a treeless land
Or stone of basalt merely there
In the abrupt water, or stone
Of the hurled meteor, stone of planet.
Strange comfort, but comfort
To all men voyaging.

We remember him,
Especially his hope for a future,
As if he had private information
On Fate's next move,
Assurances the attack would cease
At least short of his breath.
The future would be there for him,
The tides, despite their treachery
Would recede, the clouds dissipate,
The world would resume.

We know his short legs stood him
At dials, power gauges, recorders of sorts,
Stood him ignoring seas, pustular rock life,
Expectant orifice of shark,
Porpoise swaddled in a welter,
And all the rest. Was he deaf
To every threat?—the great throb
Persuasive on the steel,
Accumulative as his touch
Directed machinery to deeper reach.

He stood—so we guessed—
Very securely, and cultivated
Dreams of his achievement
In drawing-rooms and on the radio,
Of his voice rising with assurance,
Of his meeting the great,
Of extraordinary happiness in store.
God cherish him his happiness
Such strength was in that dream
That Heaven budded there.

Hammered between—these poles apart,
Water and the Word—the Fisherman.
Here his life story, his dull windy morning,
His seasonal activity, his dealing,
Sleep, worship, his world.
He stands sure footed in what universe?

Beneath boards the weight of waters
Pressures, fluctuations, varying darknesses,
Degrees of light and subtle glooms.
Above—the customary skies
Of blessing and vicissitude.
His face is tanned and set
As is a compass.

What worlds of journeys his!

Between bigotry, the simple ecstasy
And order, discipline, he swings,
Yet seeing in all things easy, difficult,
Raw or superfine, the hand of God.

Between what worlds his range!

Motion at feet and hand and brain,
In this he stands, this his normality.
Poised, and for ever dangerous,
He holds his course
Astute, reliable, brave,
Safe in the hand of God.

1   Hallo! you little sad messenger,
    Reminder of unalterable woes,
    Trespasser, your dress is inappropriate—
    A Spring bud red to blossom in snows.
    Here only are steel springs, the ayes and noes
    Of dry merchants with demand notes
    Short circuited by multiple stores.
    Go! Take your hints of country habitation
    Where the farm boy snores.

2   That sharp wisdom in your eyes
    Proclaims the hunger of centuries,
    Slips in upon even the remote heart
    Here held in city maladies.
    Your pertinent call reminds the too-cajoled mind
    That territories of Europe
    Frozen in their boundaries
    Hold beneath the skin
    The semblances of men,
    Blood runs in veins concealed.

Robins

Reminder of a world not of our making,
They have their own greeting,
Their own weeping,
Their privacy, custom and formality.

Winter compels their beggary at our doors,
But they as in court dress,
Stiff with apprehensive elegance,
Present to us their note for maintenance.

Curious that these long-overdue February flowers
Should come almost unexpected to our
Remote world: and they suspensive in cold and light
Now remain even in their proper powers

Like a legend, dreamt of, not hoped on;
Nor for us, these, delicate, of perfect leaf
And petal, but secret hold
For other Springs their promissory note.

An image on the sea's floor,
A plushy fungus, brine bubbled,
Will hold secure
(Breath and eyes untroubled),
From all uncertainties of choice
Every child that's suckled,
   And minister the fragrance
Of unstilled expectation
   And swim sweet surprise,
At every shimmer, to his eyes.

A Child Crying

The miserable moment
Breaks in your eyes
Breaks world, time, life in cries,
Spills all hope and pleasure upon the floor,
Tashes your body with the sore.

Fling a sunbeam in your eyes,
And frustrate every emblem of despair,
Cries to laughter, cries, cries, now laughter
Catch all morning air,
All sourness meadowfair.

A Young Girl

Bird eyes and voice ejaculate
Your comment
That flies uncaged
To us, stone-faced.

We watch your scattered notes
Ascend as rocket sparks
And fall like rain
On barren-ness.

Here is no continuing city
Voyage we then to islands in this
Flux of time and tide
And listen hoping for news beyond
Tide and time, and taste,
Anticipating the luscious long asked for
Fruit never withdrawn nor rotting.
    A sun shines—but where?

From prints upon the brain,
Effluent into light, the tender past—
That seen by my childhood's eyes,
That which has long since withdrawn
On an ebb—flows now.
The rocking horse with glazed eye stares,
The cuckoo clock calls,
Its door shuts—these, part of a
Once for ever world, now once
Upon a time—gone with
The silver gong's stroke, fallen
From permanence.

Voyage we for islands securely pebbled,
Holding the boat's jar, time resistant,
With water diamonded under a white sun.
But where?

The Agony in the Garden

Distant an unimportant soldiery,
(Those proscribed from bliss and agony
Living in worlds of space and time)
Sleepers, the garden of Gethsemane,
Depiction of His eyes and hands.

Look there in the garden
Where all shapes taken from
Hexagonal basalt to eruptive flame,
Prelude to the pattern
Of field and stream,
Retain, gather disruption,
Collect the flux of time and flame

  To precipitate upon
  The eyes that seek,
  The hands that ask
  The peace, the peace
  Within the eyes that plead
  The hands that speak,
  Within the balls
  The way, the life, the peace.

The short man waves his hand,
Half turns, and then makes off.
He is going to the country
Taking the road with the field of clover
On one side, the beach on the other,
The beach jarred by white stones,
The clover globed waiting for soft winds.
At the top of the rise within earshot
Of both sea and birds for a moment
He stops. (Stop now for ever there
To witness sea sound, bird note,
Sea town's cries). But he,
As if hurt and shamed,
Moves, head bent, clothes loose upon him.

We would offer blood, cash down,
For a last knowing gesture,
But the hill has him—or the sea.

Jute Spinner

What is it makes that shuttle fly?
Not ultimately the stroke of an uninformed engine,
Nor the subtle project of a capital enterprise.

What is it makes that shuttle fly?
Not a high voltage,
Nor current transmitted from a central store,
But every strand woven,
Every strand forced in
Warp and weft
Moves in its intricacy
From her nerves and bone and blood.

'Perished on the first step of tomorrow.'
Who knows his own epitaph?
'His strength gathered between thumb and forefinger,
The pen prompt to the bidding of mind,
His nose snuffing the aesthetic possibilities of the violet,
Ears and eyes trained like old soldier with a new recruit's spirit.'

Who knows his own epitaph?

The Sculptor
for T. S. Halliday

The man who handles
Bronze, clay, wood, stone,
Praises the durable,
Makes marble the moment.

Limbs, feature, muscle, palm,
The fine lines from the eye,
Supple back of animal,
(O make marble the moment!)

Bone, cheek, all tangible,
All touched by time,
Touched by the sculptor's art
Make marble the moment.

> *My love, O, my love and I*
> *Walked in a strange land,*

Sun?—yes but blocked by the whitened mist,
Sea?—but known only by taste of salt,
Land?—the scent of clover told,
And sight gave, the field brightening beneath.

> *My love, O, my love and I*
> *Walked in a strange land,*

As robins do in a farm kitchen
Leaving momentarily prints on the stone flags,
Yet we different, our eyes turned within
To the fog that swirls at the eye sockets.

> *My love, O, my love and I*
> *Walked in a strange land,*

Hearing the sea swell that runs
Brain high and ebbs, leaving us a skull.
Our flowers sprout in our aches,
And shine from our dust.

> *My love, O, my love and I*
> *Walked in a strange land.*

Where, where is the home-land?
Which, which the blessed reality?
The foam crystalling on the bowsprit,
The image heaving on mortality?

Envoi

Go, drama of wind, water and stone,
Drama of men long under granite lid.
Go to those with abundant energy
Whose eyes lift to the hard North light.
Go to those shaken by the petulant sea.

A MAN OF
INCONSEQUENT
BUILD

and other poems

1943 - 64

A Man of Inconsequent Build
In memoriam H.G.B. (1873–1941)

1 For the few only, time has gifts,
  For most, ignoring her, crack.
  They cultivate a shell resistant
  To the taps, and willing deafness
  Hear no news of death or life
  Till at the brittle end.
  But for the choice few
  Participants, patient, unsheltered,
  And tender to the fine point;
  They have time's gifts.

2 Almost bankrupted, business tied,
  The office held him to his chair,
  He sweated, hoped, lost heart,
  Yet through it noted his own suffering.
  And with this art the casual seas
  That made his trade, were legends,
  Babbled the jingling river stones,
  The flowers, that fringe the wave, stared out,
  Books with their different names
  And title deeds to recognition were grateful
  For his eye. His Odyssey the trains between
  Two ends of telephone; his giants competitors
  But these became a man who limped,
  Or interesting because he'd news from other parts,
  Or held odd notions about signing cheques.

3 The roads to the port struggle from their enclosures
  Down and flatten clear to the spatulate piers—
  Ten fingers of them seaward—
  And a long encircling wall to with-hold surge.
  To—fro in summer on a pier point coils
  Of horse-drawn lorries, klaxoned motor power lorries
  Unwind in dust in a stretch up home
  To kipper sheds and yards, and down again.
  At the dead centre a man

Manipulating the machinery of events
Sucked so far within that shipmasts,
The swinging arms, cursing ratchets,
The shafts of airward steam,
Shutter the sky. So far within—above
The Jew bargains with a closed fist,
The markets slip, dust spirals,
So far within at the dead centre
A man of inconsequent build.

4   High upon a three legged stool the small man
With broad pale brow lined deep as if the pen
Held tight in hand had pressed its ink
In strokes. The office low-roofed, flaking plaster,
And he absorbed in computation stares on ink.
(*Sleep, sleep the wound in the brain*).
A corrupting worm has fed upon the wood
Of stool and floor. He calculates. (*Sleep, sleep*).
The low white light of morning breaks
With birds, and still his eyes reflect only
What the creatures of the day have seen,
The white, the red, the gray of dawn.
(*Sleep, sleep the dust*).
Perilous, he pauses, ignorant of peril and,
With acetylene's force upon the steel, stares
On memory. (*Sleep the worm*).
Eyes open on micacious beach,
Islands assorted in their seas,
The air talk talks of gulls,
He stares without the pointed fear.
(*Sleep, sleep the dust; the wound, the worm in the brain*).

5   All held in a hand, all
Emanating from a head—God's Head,
Fish, antelope and star, held
And scattered each to his kind.
O to look equally on all, to stare

Even where His effulgence breaks in kind,
Bursts as a hurtling night
In a holocaust on a sail—
A boat broken on an ancient pier
With thrust of seeding water.
Did he learn to look
On jacket and sea-boot cast with plasm:
Watch in the beam of his intelligence
The worm in the chrysalis and the old
Woman on the stairs go from him,
And not regret their difference?

6   To see without fear, to be
A face in stillness. Latterly
Catarrhs, deafness, rheumatics occupied
His body; unconfined anxieties
Rumaged his tattered landscape.
Only his will remained in eyes
Time drawn. And then one day
The stuccoed ceiling gave, dissolved
To winter blue and in these airs
Becalmed perhaps he saw
The balance of his life—a gull
Remote and small, distinct and hovering,
Momentarily still with the apparent stillness
Of the distant waterfall; yet he at once
In the enjoyment of distance
And where his look fell,
Winged, equable, far seeing, benign, full,
As if had been projected from the body
The filled soul. He was there
Totally it and its difference.

1   The wind blows
I stare on memories
As if each breath could resurrect
The broken past.

The wind blows
Kindles the past—
The town, street, room, bed.
Head of my street—

The spire in blue,
And blown about the dusty street
The crumpled dusty leaves
The breath awakes from sleep.

2   Thus stood the father
Hand on my shoulder,
Thus the mother
Arm wound about me.

Did they ever move
From the sepia
Those in the staring days?
Reined white horses

Prance in the cold sun
Father, mother, sister,
Brother—sea-blown
On the long prom.

3   Moved they ever!
Ah pity, pity, pity,
Cried I at my entry
Wept mother,
My father in a far country.

1 TOM AND HIS TOYS

When I was small
I sat on the floor
For long, for long
And played with my golden ball.

The red engine and the black golliwog—
They sat and stared,
Stared at me till day
Dropped into the dark

That grew from the floor.
Then the tall mother moved
In the room with the great
Cupboard door. She said,

'Put them away—
The black golliwog, the red engine
And the golden ball—
Put them all away.'

She shut them in the cupboard
And never, never, never
Does the great door open,
Let them out, to stare so

As they did—this day, this night
For in the morning
I am a man.
The door does not open for the father.

2 TOM ON THE BEACH

With bent back, world's curve on it
I brood over my pretty pool
And hunt the pale, flat, sand coloured
Fish, with cupped hands, in the cold.

Ah, but my warm heart, with hope
Wrapped in it in the bright afternoon
Feet glittering in the sand,
Eyes on my pale prey, was sure.

Suns have passed, suns have passed,
Skies purple above the thin sand.
With bent back brooding on the round
World, over my shoulder

I feel the touch of a future
In the cold. The little fish
Come not near me, cleaving
To their element and flattening on the sand.

How many years since with sure heart
And prophecy of success
Warmed in it
Did I look with delight on the little fish,

Start with happiness, the warm sun on me?
Now the waters spread horizonwards,
Great skies meet them,
I brood upon uncompleted tasks.

3   TOM IN BED

Tomorrow—in the steady afternoon
When the flat sand wrinkles miles
To the bleak monstered rocks
There I shall build my mountain

Of sand, and the red crab, the green crab,
The prickly spider crab will scramble over
And will awkwardly drop
Into the prepared pool on the other side.

That is what I will do with my spare time
And should have done so
Had not the suds of a thriving tide
Pushed to my heels—and there

Behind me was the sea. And on it
The Ship—the Ship that for nights
Toppled about my bed
Carried its tarry business-like air

Its barnacles and clammy sponges
To my nose and lips. My Ship!
My venture to be—but the invitation
Held hidden the knocking first

If not carrion—and I would have plunged
Blanket wise but that the foam–
Brushed first life was there
Beneath in the child dark.

We hold out our hands to History
Then ask not to be taken.

4   TOM DISCOVERS

On our cold summer afternoons the beaches were peopled.
Then when the mothers spread their rugs on the sand
To sit and knit the long day, when the kind sea
Washed to our waiting feet the tiny sea-creatures
Everything was simple and known—the pretty shells
In the green water were still, the painted pails contained
Enough water for the shallow pools. The sandwiches
And the tea-pots, the far-off gulls,
The houses and the churches and the factory chimney stood
In that air undisturbed, unmoving in the long afternoon.

But at night I would return to a different order
The sea withdrawn shrunken grey with a grey mud beneath

Lapping those rocks—not the blue rocks
The friends of the middle tides and every boy—
But those to be seen rarely—in moonlight I remember—
Loose and piled, scarred, splotched red and black
With green fingers of slithering weed.
Once I put my hand under the weed
Aged ten—a hand of ten years—to find
Time. And at night the mirror of the mind
Took up those towered and ancient rocks
With their unseen strength and depth
Of soft weed that swayed and turned
Persuaded by the mumbling tide!
O age, age, age and a world
Thundering to the insecure stars from a hand
But ten years gone from the womb.

Boys

1   IN A CROWD

Run—
In some corner boys, men will be
Picking up their heels; in almost any
Small town on the map of our island
On a bright cold summer Saturday,
In a sea-town going to the local football match
With a crowd of blue-trousered men, all
Stockily built and lean, some bearded,
Some blue chinned, going to the big game.
They walk on the crown of the tarred streets,
Hands dropping easily at sides, or in pockets
To clicking turnstiles, or in, if they're players,
At the big gate. And not a handsbreadth off
Sunday psalms; and always about their ears
Boats bobbing, cascades of herring.

2 SEEN DISTANT

The bird perches on the corroded machine,
The derelict machine in tall spindling grass
And the wind moves from the sand landward.
We were the shabby boys that edged the beach
Till night and watched the sea-light fail,
The sand blow draughty through our legs
And coil in puffs and leap and fall,
We blowing on our blue hands
And stamping on the shore.
The birds perches on the corroded machine
The derelict machine in tall spindling grass.

Fool and Cat

1 I drove in my engine
   Along the great street
   The crowds saw me coming
   And called it a feat

   The fool and the cat
   Come into their own.

   I counted the pennies
   I counted the gold
   I piled up the counter
   With bank notes untold

   The fool and the cat
   Come into their own.

   By code and by query
   I taught in a school
   I made them all judges
   By Zeus they could rule

   The fool and the cat
   Come into their own.

I put out ten placards
They came from afar
They saw my gilt posters—
My gold cinema

*The fool and the cat
Come into their own.*

Then in came the couples
And how they did stare
My show was the best
That ever was there

*The fool and the cat
Come into their own.*

They necked and they noodled
The manager smiled—
The banker, the judge, the teacher
Beguiled.

*The fool and the cat
Come into their own.*

O sweet are the lips
That grow on the screen
And pleasant the deaths
That are done in dream

*The fool and the cat
Come into their own.*

2 My engine screams upon its side;
Who shouted in the darkening air?
A foul wind blows my notes about;
Who mocked at my despair?

*The fool and the cat
Come into their own.*

Time brought me a gold-eyed frog,
   A secretive snail, a squirrel,
A most delicate stepping high horse, and a hog,
   An ape and weasel.

Famine and drought and disbelief
   Now deny my sight
High horse and squirrel. A thief
   Took away my snail and frog.

Yet not the thickening at the eye
   Nor the thinning blood
Vanquish the trinity standing by,
   Ape, weasel and hog.

Proteus

When life breaks from the bone
Of the land, breaks in the dim
Morning, breaks in the hard known
Day, in the thin night wind,

Breaks as the heterogeneous,
Squalid, swarming plasm or
The single rock rose hid,
(Scenting a crannie's core,)

Breaks as the fact
Incredible—the babe—
Arriving in the sunless
Hut in the rubble.

Her young son singing
By her side,
Blackbird ringing
His sky-note high and wide—

Laughter over water
Where, where her heart hides
There singing sought her
Singing leaves and airs and tides.

Upon the pausing air
The leaf dry and sere
In a momentary pause
Proclaims the good.

Cleave the wood
And the moment's halt
At the axe blade's fall
Proclaims the good.

Strike the stone
And the force that stood
A moment on the stone
Proclaims the good.

The moment of darkness
Falling on the air,
The moment of brightness
Rising on the air,

Halts to a poise
The beating blood,
The beating brain,
Proclaims the good.

An Elegy for Four Airmen

To this house, here
In this town
With the past
Like a blanket
Upon it, came

Four men, to be
Air-men, to do
What youth must.
(Has done these days
With wager, laugh
Or curse).

This house—
Environed by study,
Immaculate study,
Slow-paced study—
Was *their* place.

One by one
The world-wide,
Hero-wanderers
Knew it
As home

As the moon grew,
First one;
As it waned
Another;
A third, in darkness;

A fourth—all
Into the unfair distances
Over the unkind islands
And waters, cloud storeyed
On windy ways,

To do what youth must
(These days)
Each to know
What age could not
Know.

Feather in the slip stream
Their bodies—this, only
This their discovery.
Vacancies between
The heart beats

Are greater, greater
Than the interstellar
Vacancies, greater
Than the

Outward eye conceives.
Heart convinced
Tomorrow was too far,
Each was hurried, rather
Slipped off his

Harness. Lord! what
Lonely days, months
Years in the moment
Beyond whose bound—

Now the deliberate four walls
Hold but memories. Four men
To be four air-men. All
Sweetness of life
In four known walls.

The towers by the years
Broken, are stained
By the sea's airs,
The airs that wind
About the arches,
The towers grown old
Fading upon the evening
With the sea-sound
About them; gently
The years winding
About them.

But the new
House was savaged,
A blemish; yet will it
So change, so alter
To be time-fit
No longer a halt,
The years closing upon it
Gifting the harmonies of ruin
The stillness of ruin.
Peace say the years
Peace in the stillness of the years.

At the East Port, St Andrews

Pause stranger at the porch: nothing beyond
This framing arch of stone, but scattered rocks
And sea and these on the low beach
Original to the cataclysm and the dark.

Once one man bent to the stone, another
Dropped the measuring line, a third and fourth
Together lifted and positioned the dressed stone
Making wall and arch; yet others
Settled the iron doors on squawking hinge
To shut without the querulous seas and men.
Order and virtue and love (they say)
Dwelt in the town—but that was long ago.
Then the stranger at the gate, the merchants,
Missioners, the blind beggar with the dog,
The miscellaneous vendors (duly inspected)
Were welcome within the wall that held from sight
The water's brawl. All that was long ago.
Now the iron doors are down to dust,
But the stumps of hinge remain. The arch
Opens to the element—the stones dented
And stained to green and purple and rust.

Pigeons settle on the top. Stranger,
On this winter afternoon pause at the porch,
For the dark land beyond stretches
To the unapproachable element; bright
As night falls and with the allurement of peace,
Concealing under the bland feature, possession.
Not all the agitations of the world
Articulate the ultimate question as do those waters
Confining the memorable and the forgotten;
Relics, records, furtive occasions—Caesar's politics
And he who was drunk last night:
Rings, diamants, snuff boxes, warships,
Also the less worthy garments of worthy men.

Prefer then this handled stone, now ruined
While the sea mists wind about the arch.
The afternoon dwindles, night concludes,
The stone is damp unyielding to the touch,
But crumbling in the strain and stress
Of the years: the years winding about the arch,
Settling in the holes and crevices, moulding
The dressed stone. Once one man bent to it,
Another dropped the measuring line, a third
And fourth positioned to make wall and arch
Theirs. Pause stranger at this small town's edge—
The European sun knew those streets
O Jesu parvule; Christus Victus, Christus Victor,
The bells singing from their towers, the waters
Whispering to the waters, the air tolling
To the air—the faith, the faith, the faith.

All this was long ago. The lights
Are out, the town is sunk in sleep.
The boats are rocking at the pier,
The vague winds beat about the streets—
Choir and altar and chancel are gone.
Under the touch the guardian stone remains
Holding memory, reproving desire, securing hope
In the stop of water, in the lull of night
Before dawn kindles a new day.

Old tales, old customs and old men's dreams
Obscure this town. Memories abound.
In the mild misted air, and in the sharp air
Toga and gown walk the pier.
The past sleeps in the stones.

Knox in his tower, bishop and priest
In the great cathedral, a queen's visit—
All traditional currency. Once there was
Meaning in the formula, gesture implied
Act. Now where's the life of the town?

Concurrence of event and sentiment
Confound perception! But look!
A small boat brings its morning catch,
Haddock and cod, plaice and mackerel.
Good sales! Landladies, hotels, hostelries,

Housefull! And America walks the street.
Today the train's spilling its complement
Down windy lanes to restaurants,
And afternoon—the beach, queues for
Cinema—or golf all day. Night—

History shrieks from the stones,
Knox, Douglas and Wishart,
Prison and torment.
Blind the eyes, broken the heart
Knox, Douglas and Wishart.

to Jean, my sister

Town now step into your heart—
From the fine white rabbit's skull
At the sea's edge, sea-beaten and wind searched
To the faces of men set by storm
And the hope of a haven hereafter.

Now let the misted harbour with distanced sounds,
The intermittent hooves and wheels,
The sudden vibration of the night fog-horn,
The lighthouse beam stalking about your room,
The night winds at the granite corners,

Let them all now enter subtly
And settle lightly (for these were home)
And be an air within your mind.
Once you were the girl waving goodbye
To us the way-going brothers.

Now your journeys. May all the echoes
That collect in shells, and all the ancient
Sea-sounds of the town—adding your personal care,
The moment of the puppy's bliss bearing your shoe—
Be yours unfading and without tears.

To penetrate the fuss, the shelter stir and threat,
The steamy cocoa, electric words and flickering thought
Of those who moved, raised protecting arms, or slept
And to arrive, behind the eyes, at what
Had but been guessed, was his historic bent.
He looked and noted, bringing home
The calm of rock. Was this his end—
Encrusting like the frost at the pace
Of aeons, or was the human rest
Deeper, quieter than created stone?
He looked and noted, leaving us sleepers larger
Than our aches, more lasting than our dreams.

Old grey heads, curious and stupid like the old
They came about our anchored boat
Wondering at us visitors to their ancient world
Of tides and beaches peopled with fish and birds.
On the white sands the spindly oyster catchers,
In the shallows the frantic terns,
Above the mast the heavy black-backed gulls—
All considered us, took our measure.

Every would be traveller—and who is not?
Must at the first dawn-streaked sky
Step with hope—or heartless—East, West, South or North.
Seas are between, land or doubtful sky
And painful traverse sets in motion
Heart beats to an ancient tune. Time
For a departure. O Time! One it is alleged
Once sought successfully but with too much pain.

There was a pause, a cessation of motion,
A pause in the bobbing grey heads, a pause
In the motion of water. Light fixed
The red legged oyster catchers, caught
Black capped tern and lumbering gull
In an equipoise. We looked beyond
To island upon island linked in the long
Glittering of waters—wondering where?

Now in the years between I doubt
If all was well on that bright day.
Had we but kept the bounded measure,
Ceased from willing, observation, conversation
With the self and with another,
Had we but simply been at leisure
In that suspense of fish and bird and sea
And with the old grey headed seals—what then?

Where drops the pebble silent to the sea
Where red moor tufts cliff edge
Under remorseless heaven in a chill
There spreads my silent love—O rowan tree.

At this cliff edge on the flat stone
With a little soil, open to the chafing gale
Hurt by the cruel and biting salt
There spreads my silent love—O rowan tree.

Summer ends its straining light
Blood drops pendant in the yellowing sun
Harsh leaves hanging to the chilling moon
There spreads my silent love—O rowan tree.

Touched by the calculating winter mists
Cursed by obscure and beaten seas
A derelict struck by fierce frosts
There spreads my silent love—O rowan tree.

As waters halt at this cliff base
Welter and shock inviolable stone
So you—as grasp your tough roots rock—
Halt here the heart—O rowan tree!

Rummle an' dunt o' watter,
Blatter, jinkin, turn an' rin—
A' there—burst an' yatter
Sea soun an muckle an' sma win
Heich in a lift clood yokit.
Heich abune purpie sea, abune reid
Rocks—skraichs. That an' mair's i' the dirdit
Word—Sumburgh, Sumburgh Heid.

The Old Fisherman

Girn and clash ye gangrel seas
An sough ye wun
We wha frae yer mell tak ease
Loup good herrin, loup good codlin
Noo hae done.

Skirl and yammer ower the steens
An skraich ye wun
The boatie's tae the pier heid teen
Loup good herrin, loup good codlin
We hae done.

Rax, carfuffle, shift an sweir
An brak ye lift
I wha vrocht sair i the steer
Loup good herrin, loup good codlin
Noo hae done.

But oh!—the raucle ocean's sweet
An sweet the wun
To his wha frae their ploy took meat
Loup good herrin, loup good codlin
I hae done.

Late springs this North and Spring
Is cold with sea-born air.
Wind bursts in the wide country.
By dyke and ditch the whins flare
Hares leap in the new ploughed furrs
Folk gang at the business that's theirs.

> *Andra and Jockie*
> *Scutter wi the tractor*
> *Jean's i the kitchie*
> *Dod's i the byre*
> *Fred the orra loon*
> *Chops kindlin for the fire.*

Late springs this North, hard the sun,
Caller the wind that blows to the bone.

Fingal's Cave

Eye does not penetrate but ear records
From the inner wall even the susurrus of motion,
And subtle sounds elaborated by smoothed pillars
Are orchestra with wind fall and rise,
Interlaced with murmur, knock, drive,
Shock, upon stone, and all echo, echo, echo in a vault.

Thump, your boat will end herself here
As well as on a wide sea.
Cry your heart will hear its own
Cry here as well as on a mourning day.
Call—call of bone, bird, earth, water, air
And stone in a pillared west coast cavern here.

for Henry Moore

1 In stone and in the subtle pencil line
The Word was yours—this moment
Was yours, making of the shapes of war
That tumble up the telescope end
With limbs, hair, staring eyes—one thing
To contemplate, to be borne.
The word was yours to look upon
The long shelter perspective to know
This is what I or Europe am become
And no truce will dissuade the dark.
Some in the corridor will move, some sleep,
Some raise protecting arms to waive
What is already there within. The pain
Is that on all—he who by main force
Lifted the rigid back and leaned upon the hand,
And she who slept, and he who
Too far within the tube to be seen
Distinctly, whether lying prone, supine
Or propped within the concave wall,
On all the cold insists.

O Sun (Son of God) what word to restore
From anonymity restore to diversity.
What pain to awake the numbed and hooded.
As the blood flows to the frosted limb
Will the sun now touch those,
The vindictive, the denatured, the desperate,
The eyeless, the indifferent, all who
So long ago were bereft of the garden?
Beneath the ruined moon the stone sleepers
In their countries misted with the delicate yellow dust
That sifts under the nails and lies at the nostrils.
Once the vague wind broke upon their moving thighs.

2 The present is never wholly evil
The past is never wholly good

And at this moment in the dissipation,
In the movement towards no place,
Towards no end, with no time in mind,
There is the image.

3   Summon to the mind the living image.
The running figure on the fine day,
The boy amongst boys on the broad beach
The hands at the herring shaken to the hold.

And each states I am the past
As the receding daylight arc of the tunnel
These are complete and apart:
And each states I am the past.

And the command is—define, encompass
This not that, now not then, the eccentric,
The dubious, the moving, lips shaping,
Seek the images that waylay the years.

The tree in the garden, the figure
Transfixed in Time, the babe,
The parting of raiment:
Christus Victor in the garden—
The images that waylay the years:
And trust that they will set down
Time and place, this day and this place.

4   This day and this place,
And unto Adam he said
Cursed is the ground for thy sake
In sorrow shalt thou eat of it
All the days of thy life.
Thorns also and thistles
Shall it bring forth to thee
And thou shalt eat the herb of the field
In the sweat of thy face shalt thou eat bread
Till thou return unto the ground

For out of it wast thou taken
For dust thou art
And unto dust shall thou return.

The stones were lifted from the fields
The animals driven to their holes, the land
Drained, dug, planted, the ground pieced out.
The heather was beat: the crop grew
On the hill. The paths were trod,
The people were upon the land.
> *My love, O my love and I*
> *Walked in a strange land.*

Sun! but blocked by the whitened mist
Sea? but known only by the taste of salt
Land? the scent of clover told
And sight gave the field brightening beneath.
> *My love, O my love and I*
> *Walked in a strange land*

Hearing the swell that runs
Brain high and ebbs.
Where, where is the homeland?
Which, which the blessed reality?
> *My love, O my love and I*
> *Walked in a strange land.*

To go down the years thus,
To dwindle in the narrowing perspective!
I saw two and about them
The rocks stood from the ground.
A bird flew up.
In the passage the coulter was in the soil
There were two
And one with a backward look.
> *My love, O my love and I*
> *Walked in a strange land.*

5 Homage to him who reports the kingdoms of the dead,
The place of the desert and the fire and the convulsion.
Homage to him who sets down the moment of tears,
Who carefully notes those bowed, those broken
Those estranged, those contorted by violence, those waiting,
For a new day. We are a homely people
Who fear the night, remembering only
The day when the rose bloomed in the silent sun
Or the moonlit evening on the beach with the sea
Lifting its fringes flowerlike, falling and lifting,
Or the visit of friends to tea to talk of friends.
> *My love, O my love and I*
> *Walked in a strange land.*

We desire no more than that each thing
Be as it appeared to be those years before.
Your too accurate eye makes all legend.
The bear grunts in his mountain. The ice moves.
Slowly the sap gathers to the vegetation.

O do not wake us from our sleep
With new dreams in the drumming sky.
Let the old year go in our sleep.
Valediction for an old bad year.

for Andrew Stewart

What vision his. Northward he stares
On polar suns that burst and flood
On black and blood-red water
Whose movement breaking the white light
Prismatically, spreads North and North
Salt gold and green to the cold berg's foot.

What vision his when South he looks
From sea to land, across those waterways—
Home, seen now in the perspective of space,
Men minute and shadow-like, active at their doors,
Pulling their doll-like crafts ashore.
He sees their purposes, yet hears nothing,
No pebbles' jar, no thump of boat, no shout
As rapid waters easily o'erwhelm
And run about the low decks and thrust
Aside the boats, returning them to the original sea.

Yet *he* trusting these shadows,
More real than rock, hearts perdurable
Without doubt or fear—homeward steers.

Write out the wind of his hometown
And reckon its dance, not as the impact
On a wall, but on his history.

> This wind that killed in the desert
> That slit the ice-cap,
> That blasted first life from soil,
> That chanted about the Inn at night,
> Blew winter at the Babe;

Blows to a flare the light in any
Hero helmsman's brain till his head
Above its circles—hands on wheel—
Is circled by a cloudless constellation.
His eyes are stars, his arms embrace
An unhinged world. Astride the swelling wind
In the empty dawn, in the horizon light
He becomes stature.

O Thalassa! Thalassa! Where, where
Are the winged instruments of celebration!
Where are the singers of today?
We did not know that our sea, debauched
By old men's pilferings, sullied by paddling boys,
Was not unsimilar to Homer's ocean,
Our bitter, treacherous coast reminiscent.
We did not know the music of the Ancient World
Whispered with the spindrift at our back door,
Offered its strange acclamation with wintry thunderings
For all who would hear. But we
Would not, could not, had no eyes for the dawn,
No ears for the wavering music of the wind.

> *The porridge pot is on the fire,*
> *The spelding's frae the rack,*
> *Or we can catch the tide at five*
> *Ower meat we maun be swack.*
>
> *Charlie's at the pier lang syne*
> *Tae fuel engine an test her.*
> *Hist ye, Meg, the baited lines*
> *And hist ye, lass, ma s'wester.*

'The rosy-fingered dawn'—we had no eyes for the dawn—
And the music was there waiting.
Years back—when the sun only was light
And the dark lit only by the night fires
The music waiting the singers of love and violence
Of our country, with the coasts
Fringed with the lifting and falling of waters
With the wide unmarked straths and narrow glens,
The country of the ancient inviolable rock
The music waiting for the singer
To tell the tale at the roaring night fire
To send it forward into the unborn future.

> *Drap the anchor, Charlie! Dod,*

We're tee the gruns noo
If but the weather'll only haud
We'll full the boxes foo.

But gin she blaw anither bittock
Or shift a pint to North
Nae one whiting, cod or haddock,
Nae a maik we're worth.

Here the rock strewn shore and the swift tide
Breaking the timbers of the laden boat:
Here a land of rock and little soil
But held from the invader.
What is won with difficulty is twice ours
And twice over again worthy of song,
And the songs are with the black capped tern
On the wide waters and with the swinging gull
In the rebuffed wind. Songs
In a land of the strange and the common—
The irregular crags in the green winter light,
The frozen fall in the secret corrie,
The caves with the sounding waters,
The caves of the dying birds,
The hollow hills and the deadly currents
And the slow sun rising on the ordinary landscape.
The country of low stone dykes and tractable fields,
The man at his labour in the field,
The obedient dog, the sheep on the low hill,
The woman at the baking board,
The children with blue butterflies in the hard sun
On the road to the shore.
A boy with a can of milk walks to the shore,
Returns with shining herring to the dark land.

Throttle her doon, Dod
At thon black rock

Tide's runnin' strang, Dod
We'll coup gin she knock.

A sair tyave it wis, boy
In yon black swell,
But we're hame wi' a shot, boy
Will dee us well.

In the cold of morning—as day
Stretches on the hills—the beginning,
The resumption of the tasks of the day—
The woman moving about the house,
The child crying, the cattle heaving
In their stalls. The boat goes from the pier,
The wind creeps to the wide waterways,
The ploughman drives the long furrow.
And in the prime of day—activity.
By the road to the shore in the sun
The sheep's backs are dappled with sweetness.
Happiness spreads like summer.
At night the world is in the mouths of men—
Till the flames are down and the embers ash.

Lat go that rope, loon,
Watch, she'll brak,
Smert's the word, loon,
Or she snap.

Alec John's deid.
Ae weet nicht
Slipped, cracked his heid,
Pitten oot in sma' licht.

Our coasts have no laurels—only the white dawn.
Yesterday the seas cavorted, brought
With the thin spume, Alec John's blue mitt.
Yesterday a fankled line took Sandy,
A pot in the wrinkled sand foundered Jock Bayne.

To salvage 'The Water Lily' was a fikey business—
The crew were all young men.
We did not know as the tides came upon us
And our rivers ran in spate to the sea
Our waters were touched by the Athenian sun.
Where, where are the singers,
Where the winged instruments of celebration?

Gateway to the Sea (2)
Corraith, built 1871. Innellan

This was his dream. To anchor in Time
Where the fierce salt was softened by the rose.
Spindly wrought-iron gates would welcome the wide sea,
Peace would sail into his Victorian calm,
Befriend his pale city children.
All was as he imagined.
The waters brimmed beyond the gates,
A mild surf beckoned the lilies,
The croquet lawn whispered its conversation
To the waters. The yucca prospered
In the Scottish air. This sleight of hand
That conjured four white horses,
Landau, paddle boat and the band,
Waltz and polka and the parasols
On the lawn, could it sustain
The tea-rose and the hushed waters,
Convert the embattled submariners,
Cuttlefish and crab and the sub-lit world?

Evening chimed from the mantleshelf,
The whorled shells gathered the echoes,
Roses spread upon the water,
Serenely gazed from the waters,
The faces of children looked at themselves
Sails reached up from sails,

Church and house, pier and paddle steamer
Lay tenderely there. Would this pass
With the proper way of taking tea,
With the knowledge of the right answers,
With the words not to be spoken,
And History prevail,
The jungle ocean ravage garden
And house, clad hill
And the parasols, the stock-brokers
And the tea-merchants — to leave
But a stone, a stone to say
Yes to Time?

In our day
We visited the place. It stood
With the slight green gates
At the end-of-the-world moment,
And not a parasol, not a polka.
And the whorled shells gathered
The evening light and the sea sound
To themselves in air like silk.
Was this moment another dream?

Through the glass's healing eye
Each and every to his kind,
The mauve-grey turtle heaving by
Each and every as his mind.
The star-fish to his rock,
Common crab with his rock face,
Staring cod and Peter's haddock,
Each to his appointed place
Classical leviathan here contained;
All signatories to the pact —
Content to be sustained
By a single mental act.

Blind backs to the blind sea;
Something was being said by them
In their silence, while the wind blurted about
Their stone corners that stood on stone,
And the muffled talk of waters
Fell from those shut windows.
Nothing given away about the life
That must have been, must be there
Still in the dark that moved
Inside the place awaiting return.

The rock-rose opens on the rock,
Shooting light to light.

Seaman, fisherman, who do not return
To the waiting dark, you wait now
The light of the Galilean sea to break
Like a flower on your brain again.

Gull, negligent swinging, weighting wings
On an air current over black water
In slow swell, unbroken, empty. Buffet
Hurls upwards, pressures move aside
Low in a slip-stream of air.
In that gold-orbed questionless eye
That feeds promiscuously on light,
Clean, clear or dwindling ambiguous,
The spectrum ranges from black purpling
To green water where protrudes
Skeletal remains, ship-ribs; a strake
Rakes skywards with one broad traverse
Hammered with rusty bolts—the RUBY—
Gone in the dark. Of her crew, Sam only
Was drowned and he, deep in drink,
Had glowed in many sunsets in the bar;
His jewelled accordion shone with stars.
His music mixed with the racketing winch.
'Hup!' he bawled from the slithering hold,
His thigh boots deep in squeaking herring.
Basketed he swung them skywards. 'Hup!'
And 'Never fecht your meat, man.'
These were his words. Sam had no quarrel
With words or man or self,
But with the port bow. Clumsy he slipped
Cracked his bald cranium; clean out,
But rose again—will do so no more.
Cheery Sam played the bloody squeeze box
To the moon. Now silent, salted,
He stares from all that drink.
Gull ignorant as nature, surveys,
Perches on the garboard strake.

1 Whinbush, wind-beaten, flares summer.
One statement of colour only against
Rain-leaden sky, in lea of a low dyke
In rock land and salt pasture
To the round of sea. Nothing more.
No grace here, nor riches, but authority.
Here the single lark sings in the brain
(Curtailment of life by the astringent salt),
The weasel in the wall gestures at the raging
Hare making fast for, its only month, March.
Frozen in Time they utter a way
No less than Van Gogh's chair,
Shabby with pipe and ash upon it,
And no more.
          Here is authority.

2 Present now an island with multitude,
A hundred songs at once bursting the air
With larks, tumbling pee-wits till moonrise
Where orchis lights pink, blood-red and purple
The black moors, rimmed by the imponderable sea.
In this theatre the ruined arch, the stone
Steps worn by the pious and the impious
To the altar and the kitchen. Oysters
And golden amontillado for the abbot,
Brown beer for the other orders.
Between the rose-garden and the rhubarb patch
The runnel grosses the kitchen fats
And through the slits in the containing wall
Out of the castle on the hill, the bulk
Of life, the visiting soldiery come
(From time to time engendering the village)
To accept the benedictions of the cross.
Proliferation, cruelty, processionals,
Motley and some grace.

3 All gone to rack-ruin: what with
  Invasion, reformation, deformation,
  Mildew, neglect, mould, persistence
  Of air, water, heat, cold, damp,
  Mere absence of persons until
  The Ministry of Works clocked in
  (St Aidan, St Cuthbert looked from
  The priory to the herring sea).
  'Two bob a time,' said the guide,
  'Climb the wall, that's what the bastards
  Do. Set foot on hallowed ground—
  That's their carry on, 'less I nip round.'
  Two crows sit on the arch that branched
  And broke the thin blue sky.
  'Two crows! That's 'em back
  That stole St Cuthbert's new straw thatch,'
  The guard from the castle bawls;
  'Not Sundays, Thursday's opening day,
  Pubs open Sunday—all day, all day.'
  Shuttered from the sun the soldiers
  Push their dominoes on marble tops.
  The coaches roar upon the beach.
  The girls go gay in dolly hats, ribald
  The toy trumpets shriek, a feast
  For Bob, Tom, John. Lit up
  They swelter in the westering sun.
  Tonight the red-gold horses call
  With klaxon music from the stalls.
  A few spill over on the abbey grass,
  Tom Jenkins having one too many.
  Early this mild September dark
  Sets in. Soundless the sea encroaches,
  Salt encrusts the lovers and the rose.
  Forgotten on the sand two children play,
  They build an abbey with a future
  That crumbles at the touch of tide.

The water was glass and the little fish
Sported above the clear sand.
The sunflashed ripples shot a hundred
Blisses and the boat barely nodded
Yes to plenty. This was their land.

Yesterday we visited the island
Returned to tern, gull, rabbit and plover
After the occupation by another kind,
Righteous, bearded and blue-chinned men,
Curers and fishers and women to work at the herring.

Piers grew. Hammers split the screaming
Of terns. Barrels roistered down the braes—
Empties to be stuffed with herring
By Lil, Nell, Bell, Teenie and Jeannie.
Jew and Gentile were welcome to this island.

Fifty years ago old George Bruce
(Top hat packed, in case, just in case)
Shovel beard but gentle, a short man,
Pale eyed, considering mind,
Active on his pins, stumped this island.

And it was good—all was good.
(Kirks were in his waistcoat pocket
Ready for planting, pandrops
White as sea-washed pebbles ready,
But not—not to be 'sooked' at sermon).

Britannia on her brown penny
Ruling the waves and justice
Walking on the beaches in a
Black frock tailed coat;
Law, order and some good humour

And a minimum o' sweirin
Mainly frae Chairlie wha played
A squeeze box, wheezy—a wee thing—

Wi saut watter in't, played it
For the lassies to gie them speirit.

And all was work! All a-slithering
Red-eyed, salt-scaled glut of herring
Basketed, swung by ratchet, hand winched
From hold to hands bobbing at barrels
Lil, Bell, Jean, Teenie—ho! Nellie!

Oily oilskins, a-speckle with, shot with
Blood bright scales; brine fed herring
Neat, exact packed. And elbow deep
In herring, head, arms, back in a barrel
Jeannie, Teenie, Bell, Nellie.

Bottoms up. 'God', says Chairlie
'Yon quines!'—but old George Bruce—
And all was work. Barrels dunt and deave
Till peace laps the strakes of the fat steamer
Leaving the late evening air of the island

And the girls and the gulls and the wooden
Pier. 'Wood', said George Bruce 'is not enough'
And built stone. The occupation
Was zenith. The milkwort skies
Took the thundering hammers to themselves.

The roister of barrels in the heavens,
The language of Chairlie in the heavens,
Wisps of tow in the heavens,
The faint twist of smoke—
All gathered to the heavens.

(As he left his fortifications
A little wind blew about his beard,
A white handkerchief from the stern,
Frock-coated he waved farewell).
'Maister's for hame' said Chairlie.

I found no trace of him, nor others.
The cold sun treated with the present

Occupiers, fish and birds. Terns
Inhabited the stone pier, a vantage
For sallies to the transparent water

Through which we sailed gently
Yet with more disturbance than proper
Dispersing that other order that contained
Thump and scream, roar and the faint
Birth cries of what was to become.

Advance party we were of the new
Sought for stability, had come to treat
With the politic world, the darkened
World. The cathode tube, our friend,
Was tunnelled in the concreted rock.

Antennae we were to the welded
State, invested with authority to
Dispose in chemistry, defecate to
Transparency sand, rock, bowels
Of earth such as improperly impeded

Arrangement. Guaranteed by equation,
By knowledge of the violent heart of
The matter, we sat encased in
Our transparent silence. Nothing
Could stir but was seen, heard,

Known as the movement of the hand
Is known. Distance was nothing,
Desire ordered by necessity. The rare
Jewel of single, systematised thought
Empired in the nodalled brain.

Use, the beauty of it, frictionless
And therefore never spent, a new
Kind of immortality in a muscled
Relation of instrument to instrument,
Electron to electron, thought to—

Thought of the incredible chance of
ORDER. Now grandfather praised
God for a solid demonstration
Of his order and we, can we
Praise among the irregular stars,

Praise the solitary mind that moved
From the blessed time when
The blackbird disputed the hawthorn
To tomorrow slit by knowledge,
Damned by the colding dark?

Doubt tunnels rock like wood-worm,
Makes short work of the long argument of love.
(From the springy bough of the lime tree
Her song falls to the breeding soil,
O my love dwelt in a far country!)

Doubting on a northern island
I, the antennae of the race,
Cigarette glowing beneath the lid
Of night seek a lost word
Can the lips shape 'Bless, O blessed'.

The brown land behind, south and north
Dee and Don and east the doubtful sea,
The town secured by folk that warsled
With water, earth and stone; quarrying,
Shaping, smoothing their unforgiving stone,
Engineering to make this sufficient city
That takes the salt air for its own.
The pale blue winter sky, the spring green trees,
The castigating thunder rain, the wind
Beating about the midnight streets,
The hard morning sun make their change
By the white unaltered granite—
Streets of it, broad roadways, granite pavemented
To the tall tenements, rectangular wide-walled stores,
To the kirks and pillared Assembly Rooms;
Streets with drinking troughs for the animals,
And at the port quays crowded,
Overfed with horses, lorries, men and boys,
And always and at every point
Clatter on the causies.
Business is good, will be good here
At the dead end of time. Record then
This people who purposive and with strategy
Established a northern city, a coast town
That stands and stares by the waters,
Dee and Don and the sea.

Thin ice glazing summer grass;
Here the red rowan is filched from the bough
By the cracking wind.
Sap freezes in the cold sun.

This is the East coast with winter
Written into its constitution
And so is very productive of men
Who do not wait for good
In case there is none.

They know their shortening day
Drops quick into night.
Their confidence is in knowledge
Got under duress, so
They have developed that
Deliberating and acquiring mind
That comprehends facts, and acts.

Let us praise them.
They have made the land good.

Their fat lambs dance on green pastures
That run to rock ridges,
Milch cows graze on rock top,
Sap where was perished grass
They have made the land good.
Life where was none. Praise them.

HOUSES

and other poems

1 9 6 4 - 7 0

1   Of the five waiters, white, stiff-shirt fronted
With silver trays on the tips of fingers,
At the ready with napkins as white
As their paper faces,
Four were perfect.

The fifth had a shoe-lace untied.

His waxwork tear at his eye
Registered discomfiture,
Conveyed his regret to the single customer
In the corner.

The naphthalene lighting placed the scene;
Edwardian. One
Should not shop at this restaurant
Longer than need be
But pass on to carnage.

2   1914.
He returned in 1917,
His legs bandaged in khaki,
His boots shining new polished.
Marvellous how he had got rid of the trenches.

The only reminder
Was the thin red line at his throat.

3   Now when big-brother Arthur
Stepped
Over our granite doorstep
With his soldier's Balmoral
In his hand

And we had shut the door
On the bright sea
That customarily roared
Outside
And he stood there waiting

For the mother to say
'You're home and no different'.
And the jolly father
To say
'How many Boche this time?'

I put up my finger
To touch the warm flesh
Of the hero who had
Actually killed
A man

And in a good cause.

But there was no difference
In that hand.

That August the beaches with their waves
Sang their habitual songs.

O tide of no particular moment,
Mumbling inconsequences to the pink feet of little girls,
With the hot sun on the newspapers
Beneath which soft snoring fathers puff,
And the mothers knitting for dear life—
Life not yet entered on the scene
Or about to leave; content
Spilling with the sand pies on the beach,
Sporting with the swimmers in the ocean,
In the afternoon cups of tea gossiping
To the dull air; in this fixed
Security without height or depth or thought
Let the grandmothers, mothers, fathers and little children
Be no more than themselves—sufficient,
(Sufficient unto the day is the evil thereof.)
As the beach rescue throws out his chest,
As the diver cleaves the confident air,
As the billows of great Aunt Isa

Flow into and over the deck chair
On this simple day—Hallelujah!

5   In those days
War used to be kept
Decently, as Aunt Isa said
(Like the servants)
In its place

Out there . . . out there.

6   'Oot there, oot there.'
Joe said,
'A whale's blawn; herrin's
There. Helm's doun.' Joe said.

'Haud on,' Jock said,
'Ye've cloured ma heid
On thon damned winch;
Watter ships at speed.'

'Niver fecht y'r meat, lad,
There's aye them that's waur.
Alec got his leg aff
Tween a gunwale an a wa.

There's herrin oot there, lad,
Siller for the takin:
Whaur's the spunk in ye, lad?
Ye hinna y'r father's makin.'

'Muckle gweed it did ma Da,
An him V.C. an a'.
He mine sweeped the channel,
But they couldna sweep his banes awa.'

7   Fortunately they recovered
The body of the commander.
The Union Jack fluttered a little
As the waters enclosed the coffin.

8   Jockie said tae Jeannie,
     'In ma wee box, in ma wee box,
     D'ye want tae see
     Fit's in ma wee box?'

     'Siller preens for lassies
     An a gowd locket for me,
     That's fit ye've got
     In your wee box.'

     'In ma wee box, in ma wee box
     's a German sailor's finger a' worn awa
     Chawed by the sharks
     Till it's nae there ava.'

     Dunt gaed the gun
     At eleeven o' the clock,
     Up gaed the rocket
     An the war's a' done.

9   And the Lord God said,
     Can these bones live?
     For the land is full of bloody crimes,
     The city full of violence.

The Red Sky

     Till that moment the church spire
     At the top of our street was encased
     In that blue sky. Occasionally white
     Puffclouds drove straight to heaven.
     At the foot of our street
     The Central Public School, granite,
     Also encased in blue.
     We lived in between with the
     Worms, forkies, shell-fish, crabs—
     All things that crept from stones,
     And with the daisies for company.

Each was alive and very worthy,
Just right, till I met
The curly boy with the square shoulders
Who knocked me down
Pushing his fist into my teeth.
Then a crack ran through the red sky.
From then on it was never the same.

Child on the Beach

On the shore a child picked up
The bleached skull of a rabbit,
Noted the empty eye socket,
Then ran with his joy
Till this dead shell halted
His step to hear at his ear
Miracles shout from cavities
That contained seas at work.

But age picked on me that day.
The ear was blank at that hole.
The dance of all the fishes stopped,
The tern dived oh not for fun,
The sea shrunk grey and unimportant.
Listen, be attentive to the years.
Note the thin bone structure,
Salt entered the eyeholes
To make this new thing.

1 THE BETRAYAL

But the firm sand betrayed her
And the ball spinning was caught
By the shivering sea.
Treacherous it danced her heart
Took it to its perplexity in an endless
Time streaming horizonwards.

Nor would again the flaunting sun
Tell truths of happiness to be,
Nor would those disturbed waters
Entrusted with a hundred confidences
Receive her benediction; kindnesses
Would not grow from her lips again.

The dream was taken from her.
She was no more herself. Once
The blue pebbles at the edge
Of the lemonade sea were sweets
How many years had it held
In hiding this unsupportable moment.

2 SHE REBUKES THE SEA

O my love, once you were tremendous
With a billion wonders to tell,
Tell me of tales of thin finned
Angels that went about my
Pearly feet in the sand
That snuggled the brazen
Faced crabs with pop-eyes.
Once, my love, you sent
The bubbles gold-eyed to the top.
Salt you were, you, more blissful
Than candies with your sharp
Tongue. But you
Were with the unkind Time
That took the world
To the grudging night.

In the cold spring sun
the old man sits at the door
waiting for renewal as sturdy
crocuses make way for other tubers—
narcissi. A girl lightfoot
passes him without a sign,
wordless, hurrying to byre.
The cows are waiting, warm
for her pail. Outside a small boy
pokes in the ditch for spawn.
The brilliant sky shafts
the crackling branches. Dust
curls upwards to chestnut buds.

A lark wastes song in the sky.
Day diminishes. Under
the palm of the old man
words run to his fingers,
live in his blood
warmer than summer.

Butterfly
at Rubislaw Quarry

That blue day, when the white dust paused
in the air as the chisel fissured
granite block—quarried to outlast decay,
I remember a blue butterfly
that rose from dry grasses,
lifted airy over granite edge,
over corroded machine, over chasm,
in the beam of the sun—gone.

Every moment is goodbye to every moment
but the beam of the mind holds butterfly.

Explorers

1   He rode tall into the hot sun
over the raw-grained sand
amongst the shattered rocks
that at first grew lizards
—scrub also showed life—
but when his body made a long shadow
stones were his company.

Some said his purpose was
'to explore the limits of human endurance'
others that
'his curiosity about life had gone'.
Whatever—he should have taken only
a machine into that death;
what right to dehydrate a horse!

2   After the rain the child
watched, inspected, in the sun,
drops swing along the clothes line,
stop, hold rainbows inside themselves,
clear, enlarge, hang ponderous,
then burst their birth on the ground,
again and again and again.

Light—when you come to this place—
light is falling from the sky
and the water is returning it;
the land, wrinkled and dark, a dead skin
that might crack open with no sound
and the bright water drain into that breathless dark,
lost like a single life in emptiness,
and not a tree to bless with its gentle growth,
but the bone of the world pressing through,
the stone face to which the human face returns.
Inhospitable but splendid—this North land
that tells the cosmic tale
of earth and sky and water.

Water—in the beginning a drop of water
and the light was in the water and there
each stone was shaped to be itself and none other,
each shell to be itself and none other,
each creature to be itself and none other,
peerie fish and crab and whale
seen and known and named,
yet unknown as the round of the sea.

Two Love Stories

for my daughter Marjorie

1   The old man
    is going into the dark valley
    that is his life now.
    Momentarily light falls,
    a shaft on his head and shoulders,
    as the girl meets him
    on the narrow path.

    She is a shadow to him
    as she skips off and on the stony way
    to avoid him, fumbling.

    She has come from the shore.
    She carries her bliss into the mountain.

2   On those waters a certain delicate
    pale flutter of blue silk
    under the moon
    has been known to mislead
    two into a sense of permanence.
    Pass then from the white shore
    crescent under the crescent moon
    to the lit harbour
    echoing the red and orange and green
    ship-lamps in the dark waters.
    But you will be deceived here too.

    Or is it that those years ago
    still stay awaiting recall
    when the echo of a horn will turn back
    to find the moment of making

    where there is neither time nor place.

A fat squat man with a flat nose,
Dead brown eyes, heavy lidded, slow;
Stub fingered, puffy hands held in repose
On his knees, palms turned up as if to show
Nothing is concealed. He sits on the stair
Of a granite monument, himself a Buddha in stone:
In morning sunlight, wind, rain or cold he's there
Whistling a tuneless note from his throne
For his birds, pigeons that come fluttering
And tumbling about his rewarding hands,
Devouring, gorging—like a halo—circling
About his steady head. This man
Is their unknown god who blesses and will restore
Without a sermon—now and for evermore.

Philosopher

He gathers his days
as a child petals,
looks at them separately,
then together,
turns them over,
then leaves them alone

to watch them grow
as the hairs fall from
his head.

They will arrange themselves
and look at him
when his face has taken
to itself—silence.

Old Carlo

He carries the past in his shoulders.
Light caught him and the dust
that rose from the hooves and wheels
of the ox-cart weighted with
barrels with grapes for the pressing,
caught him in the white clearing as he moved
out of the shadow of the cypress
at the end of the road
on that October day—a late harvest.

The girl at his side, granddaughter,
is going to the new school in the old town
nearby. They teach science there,
physics and chemistry. In the stone
Mary the Mother above the door
and inside the Christ.

Second Class Passenger

Leaving Florence, leaving the Annunciation,
Angelico's, top of the stone stair, San Marco,
leaving expectation, astonishment, veneration—
second class on a dry Italian day,

girl with a baby in the train.
Some time had passed between the events—
the paint drying on the wall,
a brown-eyed girl in the train.

Suddenly he tautens his neck,
makes to lift his head and you
with a single slight movement of arm,
encompassing, supporting, ease
him into sweet sleep.

Trespiano, Florence. A letter for Joseph.

Leaving you with permanence written
in the olive-leafed sky,
with the faces set
in the chemistry of paint
when Leonardo was young
and the oxen yoked to the dogma
of the stone pillars of Gropina,
whitened by the weathering sun,
a word to you, in the moment,
to fix things waiting for recognition.

When you put a house down here
in this kind of time, your walls
grow meaning from each stone,
each stone talking ten centuries,
or twenty: mentioning by the way,
the prehistory in the lizard
or the modern—Michelangelo.

Yesterday when Raphael was around
someone put a foot in the dust
at your garden's edge, firming the earth up
for the seedling olive.
This day, the tree's there still.

My attic window sights roof-topped
horizons with one gold autumn tree,
its branched candelabra lit
by quick-fire contained by earth's lid,
translated to finger tips of tree,
leaf trembling in a slight wind.
Somewhere within, the sap drives
upwards—like a flame held
in a lamp-glass drawn by the funnel—
chancing the setting bone of winter.
Somewhere a concealed bird sings.

O but this boldness is dashed,
put aside by the thin city mist,
whitening, flattening till tree
is delicate as a Chinese painting.
Without dimension, this world is quality;
like the air of a tune remembered
precisely, but long after singing.

Tree

Into a monotone sky a November tree
puts its black main-branch slimming to the top,
not vertical, but off course, the growth rhythm
one way, then subject to correction—the slow
dance of growth—the other, and each twig
starting from the tree turns and points upwards
into the blank day. All the leaves have dropped off,
the sky irresponsive and the air merely bleak,
yet each tip conveying a promise—made far below
in the black earth to the eye,
in its individual pointing upwards,
in its wayward yet controlled resilience—
of tomorrow. Tomorrow survival.
Tomorrow the sap will express itself,
in the first bud. God, if this fruit
is for this wood, why should that child
cry into her frightened night? Why
should men be computed as stones?
Tomorrow the idiot gun looks for another corpse.

Intrusion

This day, this time
when the telly grunts
in the little rooms offering sleep,
we might have stayed happy
on the old lie—time is as was,
but that outside my writing window
waterdrops slip along the wire
and pendulous, prepare to drop
their birth-bursting world.

The foetus wakes into life
with a cry.

Street Conversation

'In this wilderness, my friend—'
I said, standing on the kerb, corner
of Sauchiehall Street/Hope Street,
with the little football men returning
from their dream—Celtic, Rangers—
in the even light that swims
people and palaces (picture and bingo)
into their grey limbo. 'Watch' he said,
'you don't trip on the stank.' I said,
'Outside the wolves howl in the red-green
amber winter lights.
                        Old man, your face,
from the coal-face witnesses in favour of
the dust.'

'o.k. o.k. o.k.' he said.

Sketch of Poet
for Norman MacCaig

MacCaig angular in a wind-rainy day,
long, lithe striding to a shop;
at the lintel one step down halts;
large head swivels, toppling
eye over shoulder, stares—for what?
To pick the chemical sun from this gusty sky
to make fictions. He'll convince
parchment is split new stop-press,
crammed with the latest, liveliest,
nerve vibrating, lovely and tender
forms as enticing as girls,
as mature as malt,
so long only as the Word which is now
that spectacled old lady counter-bound,
exists. MacCaig enters shop.

Homage to Hugh MacDiarmid

(Age 75 – 11th August 1967)

After the rhetoric, the presentations,
the LL.D's, the public appearances,
the front;
       a few things worth noting.
At 8.30 a.m.
       in Princes St Gardens
the lovers, having arrived from another country
and witnessed the Scott monument,
embraced.

          'Meanwhile'
old man, you put a memorable foot
on the stone floor of your cottage
and waited for the day to catch up.
It was out there all right
breathing
       so you put it on paper
which you had done for fifty years odd.

What more's required of you
who put the breathing years in a pen.

'Little children, it is for the last time.'

and each time it was.

He spoke with his body and tongue
for love.
God knows why in our bad times.

Credibility had long since gone
that the churches had something to do with the
Christ,
that the bombs dropped for humanity;
could not deceive any longer,
even the Americans.
But that he, such as he, could for
the last
        time
and again the
                last time
for love of, for the possibility of
healing, holding together,
possibility of resurrecting
the dead god of
                love,
Walk.

The lark sings Christ in the clear air.
O Memphis. O Jerusalem.

1   Fact. Registration.

It is finished—the wall,
rough-cast and established, apparently,
and the paint tactile and the mortar there;
wall made out of your too great exertion:

                        and then
the terrible knowledge as conclusion that every
stone holds, but. B U T shakes; but holds
(to save you, us from night.)
Yet you achieve object, that, no more:
object achieved—wall. Finished
as you were in the fictive act—
to make order; order prevails
but the crevasse waits.

With this knowledge you operated without anaesthetic
on the nerve, on self and out of this willed
wall.

No more.

2   In the afternoon
a girl walked on the bright grass
outside the gallery. High noon
for her.
    She did not witness your monument.

seen on television war report documentary

He ran in the living air,
exultation in his heels.

A gust of wind will erect
a twisting tower of dried leaves
that will collapse when
the breath is withdrawn.

He turned momentarily,
his eyes looking into his fear,
seeking himself.

When he fell the dust
hung in the air
like an empty container
of him.

They had clarity.

The simple news
that it was good
to be

no more
that was enough

fingers to touch
the blank wall
enough

till that moment
precise
as the trigger.

Down the years
we did not get
the message

but spent time
as trash.

1   TOUCH

and no sound
and no word spoken
and the window pane
grey in dwindling light
and no word spoken
but touch, your touch
upon my hand veined
by the changing years
that gave and took away
yet gave a touch
that took away
the years between
and brought to this grey day
the brightness we had seen
before the years had grown between.

2   TOWER ON CLIFF TOP. Easter, 1968

When I took your hand, securing
you at the turn of the stone stair,
for the narrow step deepened by unknown
steps that climbed that dark,
(many generations in that dark
that split the day from day)
the sky broke blue above;
below the stone cube, the flat sea,
then in this place we knew
what we had known before
the years grew in us together,
yet never knew as here and now
in sudden glare and roaring airs,
as time had waited on this time
to know this in our broken day
when I took your hand.

3   LOVE IN AGE

Now that we have had our day, you
having carried, borne children,
been responsible through the wearing years,
in this moment and the next
and still the next as our love
spreads to tomorrow's horizon,
we talk a little before silence.

Let the young make up their love songs,
about which subject they are securely ignorant.
Let them look into eyes that mirror
themselves. Let them groan and ululate
their desire into a microphone. Let them
shout their proclamations over the tannoy
—a whisper is enough for us.

In the Highland hotel
the highland waiter
is waxed: in the off-season
when stags rut and their roaring
quivers the icicles from the eaves,
inside, in a ten foot tall bell jar,
in rubbed morning coat,
napkin at the ready,
his brown eyes staring from his yellow
smooth skin, preserved, deferential,
he stands waiting in his improbable world

for the incredible August people
who kill birds and deer —
and not for need.
At least he can be verified,
visible in a tall bell jar.
Of the rest who found significance
in killing birds and deer,
we only heard tell.

The marmalade is thick
with Glasgow accents.
The cornflakes flute
with Freda's giggles.

Betty and Alec go
bounce bounce
into the
cold lemonade sea

that waited the round year,
as did the soft rain
for them, dripping
and yawning into their

honey moon-suckled night,
misted: in the morning
she collected
a smooth sea stone,

put it on the step
with love;
a stone is enough
with love.

'Sunset-red rhododendrons—
to your left.' You look
with one neck. 'To your right
alone on the rock in the blue bay—
a solitary heron, the emblem
of Arran.' At the top of the pass,
'over there now hidden in the mist—
the white stag of Arran.'
With one head you look at nothing.

The little waves lap their feet
on the golden shore.
They look at nothing.

Success is to look
at nothing
be neither
yesterday nor tomorrow.

Yesterday the *Girl Jean*
running for tomorrow
with a fair catch
off Holy Isle,
struck an iron sea.
It took her and her crew
to the trash of the abyss.

Death was not their due.

A Pigeon's Feather
by Sainte Chapelle, Paris

These skies have never quite emptied
of angels.

>Tack teeth smiling pin-tables,
nickel spinning miles of
battering fruit machines, op
pop, cliff-top in plush tip-ups,
wrapped goods—is o.k. for a
smart polish in a close neon night

but these skies have never quite emptied
of angels.

>Out of that pale blue
Angelico in the Louvre
down by Sainte Chapelle
a white feather
>>floated.

>Peace,
'nostra pace'
maybe
was somewhere around.

Life risks all in that perfection
in the blown bloom, pink
in crusty snow concealing earth.
The leaf is weighted with snow.
Small comfort the windbreak wall,
but flowers open to the winter sun.

Virtue from politics of survival,
seemliness. For black and jew
strategies are necessity,
deceptions, lying necessities,
prostrations, bribes necessities.
We cherish our distorted faces,

that grimace guilt in eyes
of human hate, yet stare
with longing on that strange world
that blossoms in the snow,
growing where no life should grow
on this short winter day.

Look the Other Way

or you might see what the Pole and the Jew and the Black knew,
might discover that you were no other than he who
tortured and turned away or passed by on the other side, might
suffer the arc light of his mind whose sight you took away, whose
being destroyed; truth would destroy you—so look the other way.

Only he who with paint, stone, word, sound took out
of that Auschwitz the sad face, stricken brain, torment
for resurrection's sake (Christ's sake) for us today,
makes us whole; but you will look the other way.

The Word

1   THE SEARCH

Now all these tunnelings in the soft dark
with the sand sifting and falling as fast as
you scooped it back with hands, fingers, nails
and you on all fours like a dog, panting till you
sweat drops dropping from your forehead onto
the sand, coagulating it, giving a little hope
that the cavern would stay and you would enter
and find what you sought in that dark, what you, what
you had hoped for, but what?

or it was the ascent of the grey mountains and the dross
coming back at you sifting into your boots and you
coming down two for every three but pushing up and up
for you were the first ever on that waste—so you thought—
and you would find gleaming that hoped for bliss lying
in the ungrowing dust and the name traveller–
discoverer would shine from your forehead
as you came back from that farthest moon country

for you would bring back (ah Christ!) with all that toil,
carrying it in your hands, cupped carefully in case
it would spill or slip or fly up or vanish
and you staring at it so that it might not escape from
the beam of the mind, for over sixty years
this was your only discovery. Look and look
nor turn away or be stone (like Lot's wife) or
lose all in a twinkling (like Orpheus) all that
for which you had laboured and shrunken,
got wrinkled, bald, worn so that the lines
in your face were clefts; and this was it all,
this was what the distance of your short long life,
the running of life, the creeping and tugging, the
desperate heaving, the getting up in the morning,
the pissing in the bathroom, was—
to bring home the Word.

When they put the first man on the moon

and the dust rose about his five feet ten
he knew less than, less than that which I
had gathered, dug for, sought after with
the sweat of love, for I had worked
in the sterile deserts of brain. Sixty
years to find a, to find a, to cry out
Word.

2   THE WORD IN THE HIGH RISE FLATS, EASTERHOUSE

At Easterhouse she was pinnacled in the tinkling skies
high, so high—as she did her nails in the pink morning—
she saw onto the Lochs and the Lomonds in her pin-up head
and heard the sweet guitars of Balloch as they swung
from the golden shore into the blue ice-cream loch
with their honeys for bliss. In these skies,
while the patch, sixteen storeys away screamed with
the blood of councillors and bus drivers and what not,
he planted his seed in her soil.

As smooth, as bright as chromium, all her days glittered
in her nine months sunshine, and not a doubt on the horizon
for FLAT 2007a, sixteen floors up (one down, the intellectual
roamed his Borroughs fackwords and borwards—and no outcome)
but *their* word was flesh, and straight, flash-Bingo!
seven garden dwarfs, two cocktail cabinets and color telly
were his—him straight from her plastic womb up there—
all his, who would never smell the sour smell of the
breeding earth.

And the product of her parturition, from the dumps
and dunnies, grew teeth, razors, chains, flick-knives,
to comfort his solitary confinement in the flesh.
And the dust rose from the long shitten dry yard
about his eyes, he hugging the smoke from the fagdowps
about him, 'case he might know himself from her,
him from him, her from him, might know self, know
he was one, one alone in the breathing night; so—
Ya! Bass!

O lily perfumed lady of the chromium bower,
bearer of the cup of sweetness and of light,
that minister'd him to that sweet sleep
but yesterday; but meth, but pot,
now bear his cares away.
Come down, o goddess from the pearly sky
and sing a lullaby, lulla, lulla,
lullaby, lulla, lulla—
grow love down here.

3   THE WORD

A hand up to touch on an airy day a small blue butterfly,
not knowing why, nor where, nor distance, here, there,
nor word to know what, but look sensing the moment of now,
when no time is, the hand up to touch, clutch
nothing, not knowing space, but in space he is,
space-belonging before time claims his coming.

Belonging? Being—his being is when she only,
smoothing the pram cover, moving at an angle
to give food, shelter, covering; when she is bending
as an arc of sky round world's curve,
bends over—her warm shadow is day to him—
she is Word to him, day and night word.

Our night—the myths creep to their holes.
The sky is a hole. Freud dug his garden
and the serpent became worm, and the worm was earth.
Humus, in the beginning a garden,
in the end magma.
In the beginning and end, the Word.

And every winter on the stone sill
supported on two wires that splay till
they become four springy toes at rest;
the red burns upon the breast,

bringing into the ordinary dying light
into my constructed code
your being that stains the snow
and will not let our guilt go.

Quixote in a Windmill

He saw it hoisting itself from salt marshes
into his trembling sky. It stood
on the edge of water-meadows turning
to marram grass turning to sand only
and then shallow pale sea.

He looked at the broken webs
that cracked but did not move.
Once this castle was his when
the wind bawled about, the sails
whirled in the turmoil of his mind;

racketing, squealing, grinding, they became
his madness: he watched his brain lifted
to the brazen sky, thrown down on stones—
he was King for a howling winter
till the soft Spring came and flowers.

For years
a schoolmaster looked over my right shoulder
in case my punctuation went wrong.

For years
a minister looked over my left shoulder
in case I committed a moral solecism.

They've gone.
Now I watch the sparrows in the green grass.
'Lechers!'

Reflection at Sixty

Thunder knocks about the house,
tries doors and windows.
Night. I listen in bed.

Somewhere around
there's a birth going on
that concerns me.

At Bridlington Spa
my wax moustachioed purple uncle
used to sway in the salted breeze.

'Give it up,' he said,
'All this bother about meaning.
Douse lights and out.'

'Christ!' said the surgeon, 'It's not there.' Though why
he should have expected it, considering
my heart has been in my mouth for years.
So there they were scouting around,
pulling up the tripes, chasing along the long gut,
digging the bowels, hugging the liver,
freaking out the lungs, inspecting the duodenum—
and nothing in sight. Zero hour and the trumpets
sounding. 'Christ!' said the surgeon, still doing
his nut on the wrong tack. The trouble was
semantics. Shouldn't he have known
—O Lamp of Licht—
Christus Victus, Christus Victor,
Kyrie Eleison—the water of Babylon.

Somewhere along the computerised line an omission.
Feedback. Reprogram: LLLLLLLLLLLLLLLLLLLLLLL
liblibliblibliblibliblibliblibliblibliblibliblibli
'Got it' he said. LIBERAL STUDIES.

Writing after midnight,
a slow fire going out,
cold settling in;

reminders and questions.
Now we've got moon dust in containers
there can be no more lunatics.
Remove that word from the vocabulary,

and think of Town Councils,
impeccable in their honesty,
undeviating in their purposes,
beautiful in their opacity.

'It is essential to keep things circulating,
a road to keep four wheels circulating.'
They circulate.

'It is imperative to build twenty storeys vertical.'
They build twenty storeys vertical.

I pay my tribute (exacted)
and regret the loss of a word.

1   Suddenly our house went up in the air.
    The slates, rafters, chimneypots, masonry
    burst out like a gust of starlings
    and stopped 30 feet up.
    They then decided to come down again.

    That was 1941.
    I believed my mother was inside.

2   In Edinburgh houses come down.
    Without giving notice the cement balcony
    of a council tenement left its assigned
    position
    and made a new map on the pavement.

3   Our house is different; it is very old,
    it creaks a bit in the wind,
    is water-tight now and then,
    comfortable for mice with good runways:
    it should do my time.

1 KEY

Two hands it takes to turn in the lock
and every night squealing, juddering till
it's home, locking them out, us in,
the dark out, the stream in the dark
that goes through the city carrying
what's jettisoned from life.

Two red candles on the mahogany table.
The table reflects our faces; pale
transparent we present ourselves
to ourselves at the agreed age, mature.
But who is that old man on a stick
who looks at me from the mahogany?

2 THE BIG ROOM

In our house I light the fire in the big room
with paper, sticks and matches. It heats a small area.
I sit close, holding out my hands, spreading fingers
to the flames; they become transparent, the bones
shadows beneath the skin. The fire throws shadows
on empty walls — cold out there.

Black and yellow out there. The big-eyed children
stare. Some are at the breast, some by the mothers,
seated row on row on the floor. No room elsewhere.
Our house is built of stone to shut out —
I look into the fire. The mothers hush their hunger,
whispers rising from the floor. Today

I fed the bird with Christ's blood on its breast.
He came to the sill out of blank December,
stayed for bread, now claims this territory his,
interrogates my eye, bawls out the sparrows,
allows none other (Qui s'excuse, s'accuse.)
The children's breathing comes about me cold.

My faults domestic; failure to keep the fire,
to shut up house; confess to having swept

crumbs under the carpet—matters of little consequence.
Dinner is served at eight. On the mahogany
the knives are table knives, red candles, goblets—
domestic rites, no sacrifice intended.

Perhaps one day they will go away,
run into their yellow sunshine.
In the church I shall take a collection,
'for the poor brown people far away.'
The walls sweat. 'Rising damp', they say.
Don't mistake me. We never had the torturer here.

3   THE BEDROOM

Here her apple-green dream in high summer.
Cornucopia. Lawn curtains lifted and fell.
From her virgin bed, in oes, in spangles,
in to-fro runs mingling lights and shadows, water
mirrors itself on the ceiling, a shimmer
from the slipping river running by the green plot,
her garden below. Bird voices of children.
'I am on my swing and swing so high
that the bright sky brushes my eyes.'
And over the wall where the stream
is glass the swan placed to be seen.
Untouched by tomorrow or yesterday
tea will be served on the lawn
and afterwards, chocolate creams.

4   THE STUDY

I secrete myself between two commas with
Jonson, B., Marlowe, C., Shakespeare, W., Webster.
My banker Uncle said: 'Poetry gets you nowhere.
Give it up. Besides . . .' Byron fornicated,
Shelley ran starkers in a drawing room,
Even Wordsworth once got a girl with child but
'that was in another country, and besides
the wench is dead.' 'The small fly goes to't.'

'Birth, copulation, death. Birth, copulation, death.'
'O lente, lente, currite noctis equi.'
Shut the book. Too many indignities.
The Bank must be protected from life.

5 THE NURSERY

To write my first word
I was set at my little table.
There would have been no difficulty
but that I felt the ogre's head
move under my feet. It threatened
to roll out from under, creating
acute adult embarrassment, a trauma.
(One has no wish to alienate,
stretch the credibility gap at age eight.)
What they cannot understand is that the gaoler,
clicking her needles, counting the stitches,
at the ready to drop one when the next head
falls, put there for company, (they say.)
adds to the overcrowding. I have already
to support in this place the woodcutter,
charcoal burner, witch and potions
serpent and tree, one bird of prey,
the dwarf, his ape, weasel and hog,
a gold eyed frog, one mandrake root,
one buried heart, one red rose with dew,
one glass mountain with princess,
one with no name. The conditions
for attention to the word were becoming
unfavourable. Correction—fortunately
it was butcher meat under my feet,
slippery under the texture of the sack.
When she complained the light was going
I was grateful for her momentary inattention.
(The floor boards creaked. The river was high.)
She said: 'Last night the shadow of a man

crossed the window, but say nothing of that.'
As if—but the blood was oozing
through the sack on to the soles of my feet,
dripping on to the floor, silently; mercifully
as long as the condition was private to me,
—she could have her sex—it was possible
I might still deliver the goods, write
down the word for which they waited
patiently and calmly in their place
of order and disbelief. For them
the river runs by the garden wall,
the rose bush is pruned in the spring,
the green swing untied for me.
For them the silver knives lie on the table,
the candles, red napkin, the goblet,
each in its appointed place and when
the clock chimes from the mantlepiece
when I have put on the white paper
their word—they say—I shall play,
but the beast kicks in the sack.
What did they do to the wound under my feet?
The wind rumbles about the corners of the house.
The little match girl in the weak light
warms her hands at the last match.
She glows in the garden like a tree
by the sick rose and the water.

Some days words come at the run
like boys for supper.
Clean and firm
they present themselves
alert and at attention.
These days are worth waiting for.

A Song for Scotland. *'the dead herring on the living water'*
A reference to those occasions when the fishermen dumped the herring back into the sea, having considered that the price offered for the catch was very inadequate. When this action was repeated by many boats it was done in the hope that the shortage of fish thereby created would result in higher prices at the auction of the following day's catch.

Sea Talk. *'being a cranner'*
Eight baskets of herring equalled the measure of one cran. The cranner was an employee of the buyer of the fish who counted the baskets as they were swung from the boat to the pier. He was responsible for seeing to it that each basket was full to overflowing and for noting that the quality of the fish was similar to what the fisherman had shown to the buyer as a sample of the catch. He also saw to it that the fish were heavily sprinkled with salt before they left the pierhead. He was therefore intimate with both sides of the business, would not be given to sentiment yet was known to express admiration for the honesty and character of the fishermen. The poem is written from a cranner's point of view.

A Man of Inconsequent Build
H.G.B., Henry George Bruce, my father, was head of A. BRUCE AND COMPANY, the oldest herring curing firm in the North of Scotland. He had no interest in making money, beyond acquiring the basic necessities of life—food, books, clothes. He is also described in *A Departure*.

Sumburgh Heid
The rocky headland at the south of the Shetland Isles. The poem is largely onomatopoeic, being descriptive of the sounds and atmosphere about Sumburgh Head. 'lift clood yokit' a sky with clouds linked together. 'dirdit'—buffeted.

The Old Fisherman
v.1: 'Girn' complain. 'clash'—not simply beat together but also 'talk' and 'gossip' as a 'gangrel' or wandering tramp would do. 'mell'—mêlée.
v.2: 'steens' stones. 'teen' taken. The verse describes the disturbance of the sea by the wind.
v.3: Continues the description—'vrocht' wrought hard in the stir of the waters.
v.4: 'raucle' rough.

Valediction for 1944
The opening of the poem describes one of Henry Moore's shelter drawings.

The Singers
The quatrains in Scots describe the fisherman's day and accident. Breakfast consists of porridge and a 'spelding frae the rack', dried fish (haddock or whiting) taken from the rack, on which they were hung. 'meat' over our meal we must be quick. Meat in Aberdeenshire refers to food in general.
'tee the gruns', close to the fishing grounds.
'full the boxes foo', 'u' pronounced as in dull, 'fill the boxes full'
'pint' point, 'maik' halfpenny.

'sair tyave' sore labour, 'shot' catch.

'pot in the wrinkled sand' a deep hole sometimes causing suction.

Fishermen's Cliff Houses

This poem was written as a response to a painting by Anne Redpath.

Cheery Sam

'Never Fecht your meat, man.' Do not quarrel with your job.

Landscapes and Figures

The first section describes an Aberdeenshire landscape. The rest is Holy Isle—Lindisfarne. There is a legend that crows stole the thatch from the roof of St Cuthbert's cottage.

The Island

My grandfather, George Bruce, was one of the earliest herring curers to set up a fishing station in Baltasound.

Aberdeen

'The Assembly Rooms', now known as The Music Hall, was built by Archibald Simpson, Aberdeen's most distinguished architect.

A Pigeon's Feather

On Ember Day, 18 September 1968, after viewing the *Coronation of the Virgin Mary* by Fra Angelico in the Louvre, my wife picked up a pigeon's feather near La Sainte Chapelle.

Sea Talk, Glasgow, Maclellan 1944
Selected Poems, Edinburgh, Saltire Modern Poets 1947
Landscapes and Figures, Preston, Akros Publications 1967

Some poems in this collection have appeared in the following books:
A Book of Scottish Verse (World's Classics), *Contemporary Scottish Verse: 1959–69, Honour'd Shade, Modern Scottish Poetry, Poetry Now, Poetry of the Forties, Scottish Poetry 1–5, The New British Poets* (USA), *The Oxford Book of Scottish Verse, The Penguin Book of Scottish Verse.*

Other poems have appeared in the following journals:
Aberdeen University Review, Blackwood's Magazine, Contemporary Poetry (USA), *Life and Letters Today, Lines Review, Poetry Scotland, Scottish International, The Aberdeen Press and Journal, The Modern Scot, The New Saltire, The Saltire Review, The Scots Magazine, The Scotsman, The Scots Review, The Scottish Field, The Voice of Scotland.*